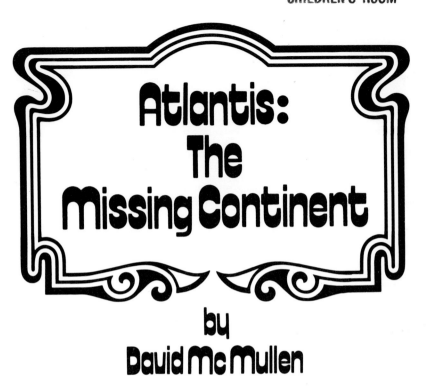

Atlantis: The Missing Continent

by
David McMullen

A
cpi
Book

From
RAINTREE CHILDRENS BOOKS
Milwaukee • Toronto • Melbourne • London

Library of Congress Number: 77-22138

Art and Photo Credits

Cover photo, Eric Schweikardt.
Illustrations on pages 7, 11, 29 and 37, Jeffrey Gatrall
Map on page 17, Courtesy of Alfred Fusco
Photo on page 18, from "Children of Mu" by James Churchward,
N.Y. Public Library
Photo on page 21, Jerry Frank, dpi
Photo on page 20, Elizabeth H. Burpee/dpi
Photo on page 23, Alinari—Scala
Photo on page 25, from "The Mystery of Atlantis,"—Berlitz, Courtesy of Comisão
Regional De Turismo Dos Açores
Photo on page 26, from "Without a Trace,"—Berlitz, Courtesy J.M. Valentine
Photos on pages 30 and 33, The Granger Collection
Photo on page 32, Courtesy of the Hispanic Society of America
Photos on pages 41 and 42, Comissão Regional de Turismo Dos Açores
Photo on page 46, Dimitri Rebikoff/International Explorers Society
All photo research for this book was provided by Roberta Guerette and
Sherry Olan.
Every effort has been made to trace the ownership of all copyrighted material in
this book and to obtain permission for its use.

Library of Congress Cataloging in Publication Data

McMullen, David W   1939-
   Atlantis: The Missing Continent.

   SUMMARY: Discusses Atlantis, the mysterious missing continent
believed to be located off the western coast of Africa.
   1. Atlantis—Juvenile literature. [1. Atlantis]
I. Title.
GN751.M26   398'.42   77-22138
ISBN 0-8172-1047-4 lib. bdg.

Manufactured in the United States of America
ISBN 0-8172-1047-4

Contents

Chapter 1
  The Dream   5

Chapter 2
  Looking Behind the Dream   15

Chapter 3
  What Was It Really Like?   23

Chapter 4
  Where Is Atlantis?   35

Chapter 5
  Is Atlantis Rising?   44

Chapter
1
The Dream

The young girl was about to go to sleep. But she was afraid. Every night her dreams were filled with the story of Atlantis, the lost continent. Every night she dreamed she was the beautiful Salustra, Empress of Atlantis. As she closed her eyes, she knew at once that Salustra was not far away. . . .

Salustra stood before the window of the Palace and sighed. It seemed that everything she loved most was dying, and she could do nothing about it. Behind her lay her father, the Emperor, in his last hours of life. He had led a fuller and longer life than most. But at the age of 200, he had decided to die. She looked back at his weak body lying on the couch, but no tears came to her eyes. Salustra never cried.

She turned to the window and looked out over Atlantis. Like a plant cut off from the light, it too was dying. The terrible yellow smog crept over everything, hiding the sun. Below Salustra, Atlantis was still. The scientists of Atlantis had long ago stopped burning coal and oil to get their energy. They had found that atomic power was too dangerous. The sun, alone, was used for power. *Everything* was driven by this solar power.

Nothing worked or moved below her. The air boats were still. So were the ships in the great harbor. The television and telephones were silent. Even the heating and cooling systems were shut down.

Salustra wiped the sweat from her forehead. She stamped her foot in anger. When would someone do something about all this? When would the smog disappear? Her thoughts were stopped by a call from her father. She went to his side and held him in her arms.

6

Salustra looked sadly over her dying city.

"Salustra?" The word came in a whisper.

"Yes, Father, I am here."

"Into your hands I place my empire—my Atlantis——"

"Hush now, Father. Rest."

"No, Salustra. I will not live long now. Atlantis is a jewel. Guard it well. Our land is old and has lost its hopes and dreams. Atlantis has become lazy. Our people want only pleasure, forgetting they must defend themselves with truth. Take care of Atlantis for me."

These were the Emperor's last words. He died in her arms soon after. The doctor felt the thin wrist of the Emperor.

"The Emperor is dead," he announced. "Long live the Empress!"

At this point in the dream the young girl stirred and turned over in her sleep. She had this dream many times before and knew what was coming. Yet, every time she dreamed with greater and greater detail. She sighed deeply and her dream continued. . . .

Atlantis was being smothered to death. No one could do anything about it. The greatest scientists simply scratched their heads sadly and looked lost. They had depended on the sun. Now it was all but blotted from view by thick blankets of smog. Who would have thought that the sun could be taken from them?

A long time ago, they had used fire, oil, and coal for their power. But when Atlantis was attacked by dinosaurs, they needed a more powerful form of energy. They found the energy and with it a way to defend themselves from the dinosaurs. The scientists exploded a terrible new kind of bomb.

One minute there was an army of dinosaurs, the next day they were gone. And so were the hills where they had stood. All that remained were some glowing red crystals. Those crystals were strangely able to make people young again. That was how the Emperor was able to live 200 years. But only a few people were allowed to use the crystals. It was the highest honor in Atlantis. Yet, not many people wanted to use the crystals more than once. It seemed that being able to die was as important as being able to live.

The scientists had warned that their new bombs would someday burn up all the air, making life impossible. Because of this, the bombs were banned from use. Atlantis grew and became the most powerful and richest nation on earth. Much of its wealth was used to make new weapons that kept the enemies of Atlantis away.

Life in Atlantis became too easy. The dying Emperor had warned the people, "Don't forget the goodness in life, just to keep the good life." But, like some children, the people were spoiled. They no longer thought for themselves. They depended more and more on their leaders.

Many people blamed Salustra for the yellow cloud that was choking them. She was responsible! She was a leader, so she should do something about it! There were rumors everywhere. Their enemies, the Althrusti, were coming. Their agents were making trouble in every part of Atlantis. Salustra was very worried. She had heard the rumors, too.

The Althrusti *were* coming, but Salustra could do nothing. Without sun power, the country's radar didn't work. Neither did the laser beams. Atlantis's warships were stuck in the harbor, blinded by the smog.

Then, one day the invasion came. The great steel warships of the Althrusti slipped through the smog into the harbor. The Althrusti were a strong, rough people used to the bitter cold of the north. They stormed through the country.

The Althrusti captured the palace.

After all those years of jealously watching their rich neighbor, Atlantis was finally theirs. Without the power of the sun, the Atlanteans were helpless.

Atlantis gave up without a struggle. Salustra was taken prisoner. She was led to the ship of the enemy leader, Signar. The captured Empress asked Signar about the horrible yellow smog and about some loud, rumbling noises that had been heard throughout the land.

Signar laughed at Salustra's questions. He had no idea what the smog was. He knew only that it had helped him capture Atlantis. That was all he cared about. As for the great rumblings from the north, he too had heard them. He didn't know what they were. Just then, they were shaken by a great noise. It was an explosion and it was not too far away.

Everyone, including Signar, felt the chill of fear. Some laughed nervously, but others gave a little cry. Then, there was a loud scream from the lookout. Roaring straight at them was a giant tidal wave. It was higher than the highest building in Atlantis. An instant later, the ship was swept up by the rushing waters. Whipped high into the air, the ship was somehow thrown clear of the crushing wave. Atlantis was not so fortunate.

One moment Atlantis was there in all her beauty. Now, the earth had cracked open and swallowed it. What was not swallowed was drowned beneath the huge wave. When the wave had passed, Atlantis was gone—its people, its buildings, and its power disappeared under tons of ocean water. It was as though Atlantis had never been at all. For the first time in her life, Salustra began to cry.

Signar and Salustra began to sail, looking for land. After a few days they found a strange wooden boat—an ark. On board was an old man, his family, and many animals. He told them he had been warned about the flood and had built the ark to survive. He said his name was Noah, and he. . . .

The dream came to a sudden end, as the girl awoke. She decided to write a book about her dream of Atlantis. The story she wrote lay hidden for nearly 60 years before it was finally published in 1976. The young girl had gone on to become a famous writer. Her name is Taylor Caldwell. The complete story of her dream is told in her book, *The Romance of Atlantis*.

Many people have dreamed of Atlantis. It was a place of peace and wisdom that some believe existed 10,000 years ago. *But did this great land ever exist? Was there really an Atlantis? Can we find any traces today?*

That is what we will explore in this book. But be warned—there are few answers to the questions you may ask. *You* will have to decide about most of the mystery called Atlantis that still baffles the world.

Chapter 2
Looking Behind The Dream

There are many strange things about Taylor Caldwell's dream. First, why should a young girl dream about Atlantis? Had she been told stories by her parents or teacher? How did she know what Atlantis was like?

There is another strange thing about the dream. Taylor Caldwell was just 12 years old at the time. Yet, she describes things that hadn't even been invented when she was 12. There were no air boats, no lasers, no televisions or radar. How did she know about all these things? You can add this mystery to the long list of strange stories told about Atlantis.

Was there ever such a place as Atlantis? Or, like the dragons that breathe fire and the unicorn, is Atlantis just a legend? Can we find proof that Atlantis ever existed? If so, where was it and what was it like?

Our very first clue to the Atlantis mystery is more than 2,000 years old. In those days history was not written, filmed, or televised. It was told in stories passed from father to son. If you wanted to know what happened in earlier times, you didn't go to the library. You went to wise old men. You listened to their stories. The Greek philosopher Plato wrote the story of Atlantis as it was told to a Greek named Solon.

Solon traveled across Africa from Greece to talk to the wise men of Egypt. Egypt, at that time, was the oldest known civilization. Solon

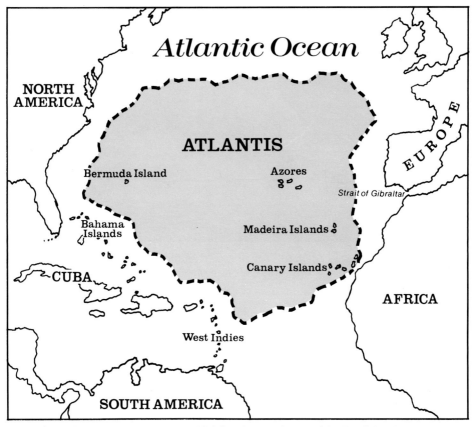

The Egyptian wise men said Atlantis was located in the Atlantic Ocean, beyond the Strait of Gibraltar.

asked about the great flood and about Noah and his ark. The wise men told Solon that the Greeks came from what was left of a much older nation. The wise men told him the people of Egypt had records that were over 8,000 years old. These Egyptian records told the story of Atlantis—a lost continent.

17

Discovered in Ancient Troy, the Bird Sphinx is inscribed: "From the King Chronos of Atlantis."

Before the flood, the wise men of Egypt said, there had been a great island. It was larger than North Africa and Asia Minor put together. This island had been off the coast of Africa in what is now the Atlantic Ocean. It was just beyond the Strait of Gibraltar, guarded by the great Rock of Gibraltar. The island had been called Atlantis.

It seems that Atlantis was ruled by a series of great and wise kings. Atlantis was looked upon by outsiders with love and envy. Whenever its neighbors were attacked, the armies of Atlantis came to their aid. Everything went well, Solon was told, until Atlantis was struck by earthquakes and floods. Volcanoes erupted and rocked the island.

Then, in one violent day and night of destruction, most of the people were swept into huge cracks in the earth. When the quakes and tidal waves passed, the whole island of Atlantis had vanished beneath the sea. The old men went on to say that the sea beyond the Strait of Gibraltar was still blocked and made it difficult for ships to pass. The shallow waters were caused by the island as she settled down into the ocean.

Those Atlanteans who survived the flood went to North Africa and Greece. It may even be that the great pyramids and the Sphinx of Egypt came from the minds of these survivors. The Atlanteans are thought to have used the sun as the source of all energy. Early Egyptians worshiped the sun and called it the god Ra. Did the Egyptians learn of the sun's greatness from the Atlanteans?

The early Greeks built beautiful buildings at a time when the people of France, Germany, and Britain were still wearing animal skins and living in caves and huts. How did the Greeks

This Greek Temple at Sounion is dedicated to Poseidon, god of the sea.

Did the Atlanteans instruct the Egyptians on how to build the Sphinx and the pyramids?

move so far ahead of the rest of the world? How did they put up such beautiful buildings?

There is no definite answer known, but the tale of the wise men in Egypt offers one possibility. Perhaps Greece and Egypt grew from the wisdom of the Atlantis survivors.

21

So, Atlantis might seem to have been something more than a dream. It may have been a real place, a huge island that sank under an ocean. But what was life on Atlantis like? What do the wise men's stories tell us of Atlantis? It may have been an advanced civilization far ahead of any that has grown up since Atlantis disappeared.

The stories we know of Atlantis were left to us by Plato, the Greek philosopher.

Chapter

3
What Was It Really Like?

Plato tells us there was an Atlantis. *It did exist.* But Plato goes even further. He takes us right into Atlantis and tells what it must have been like to live there.

He says that Atlantis was an island just off the west coast of Africa. Life there must have been closely tied to the sea. Plato describes a large, flat area of land in the middle of the island. Its soil was rich and filled with many types of plants. There were running streams, birds, wild animals, and beautiful flowers. There were great numbers of fruit and nut trees.

Atlantis must have been a wonderful place—more beautiful than anything Plato had ever seen. It sounds very much like the Garden of Eden. You know most legends are based upon real people or real places. Could it be the Garden of Eden was based on the beautiful Atlantis? We'll never know, but it's fun to think about.

Next to the flat land of Atlantis was a mountain with springs of hot mineral water that was said to be healthful. It seems that taking mineral baths in Atlantis was quite popular. There were supposedly many such baths all over the island. Atlantis was also very rich in metals like gold and copper. There was so much gold that it was used to cover buildings!

The Atlanteans put many kinds of animals to work. We are told that one work animal was the

The hot springs in the Azores, off the coast of Portugal. The springs described in Atlantis may have looked like these.

elephant. We also know there was no shortage of things to eat in Atlantis. Plato mentions the sweetness of the grapes and another fruit that had a hard rind and a rich inner flesh. That fruit gave meat to eat, juice to drink, and also an ointment. Plato was probably describing a coconut!

25

The capital city of Atlantis was on the east coast. It was built on and around a small mountain, surrounded by three rings of water to guard it. The three rings of water were like a water highway system. This made it difficult for a land army to attack the city. The inner water ring was about 600 feet wide. The largest, the outer one, was almost 2,000 feet wide. Linking the three water rings was a complicated system of canals and locks.

Are these underwater stone walls at Andros Island, off the Greek coast, from the capital city of Atlantis?

They were built wide enough to let great sea-going ships pass from the outside sea into the innermost part of the city. Plato says that there were many ships on the canals and waterways bringing trade and people into Atlantis.

The place was alive with noise, color, and motion all the time. Around each of the water rings was a great wall with towers. The Atlanteans were obviously not living calmly and peacefully. They built their city so that it could be defended against attack.

At the end of its life, Atlantis was a place of rich traders. They lived at a time when there was no law. When you wanted something you just took it. When you wanted to keep something from being taken, you had to defend it. This doesn't seem much like our dreams of Atlantis, does it? It doesn't sound like the Garden of Eden. But this is what Plato took from the stories told by the old men of Egypt. According to Plato, this was Atlantis before the great flood.

At the top of the mountain, in the center of the city, stood the temple of the god *Poseidon* (later called Neptune). Poseidon was the name given to the god of the sea. The temple had many towers and statues, all covered in gold, silver, copper, and ivory. The temple was like something from a fairy tale. It must have been quite a sight, all gold and silver sparkling in the sunlight.

The Atlanteans worshipped Poseidon as a god because of a legend told about him. It was said that Poseidon came out of the sea to become the father of the first Atlanteans. He had ten sons, five pairs of twins. So Atlantis came to be. It was made of ten regions, each ruled by a king descended from the first ten twins. The most famous king was *Atlas*. Later, in Greek mythology, Atlas is shown holding the world on his shoulders.

It was from Atlas that Atlantis got its name. And from Atlantis comes the name of the Atlantic Ocean. Atlas and his descendants ruled Atlantis from a palace built around the temple of gold and silver. Royal soldiers ringed the palace to protect it. The royal city had an army of about 60,000 men and a navy of 20,000 ships. That was only the royal city! Each of the other nine regions of Atlantis had its own army and navy. That was a lot of people just for protection! Even today it would make Atlantis a

The Atlantean Temple of Poseidon is said to have shone with gold, silver, copper, and ivory.

"superpower," almost like the strongest countries of the modern world.

Plato also tells us about the life of the people in Atlantis. The rich had a life filled with fine clothes, good food, and beautiful jewelry. They spent their time at the mineral baths and at play. The rulers of Atlantis came from the ranks of the

Atlas, descended from Poseidon, is often shown carrying the
world on his shoulders.

rich. The not-so-rich were less lucky. They found themselves in the army or navy, protecting the nation's wealth. This couldn't have been fun. As a sailor, for example, being chained to the oar of a sea-going ship doesn't sound like an easy life.

So we know that life in Atlantis was beautiful only for a few. For the others it was slavery. But life for all must have been violent. For example, every six years, the kings of Atlantis would gather in the Temple of Poseidon to honor their god and to decide the affairs of Atlantis. First, they burned ten bulls as a sacrifice. They then splashed some of the blood on the temple walls and drank the rest.

For the Atlanteans, the bull was sacred, much like the cow is today in India. Killing the bull was a religious act (although the Indians would never harm a cow). Today in Spain, there are still bullfights in which the blood of a bull is sometimes spilled in a kind of ceremony.

Spain must have been very close to the shores of Atlantis and almost certainly under its control. Could it be that the ceremony to Poseidon in Atlantis was the beginning of the Spanish bullfights? We may never know but perhaps the Spanish bullfighter of today is all that remains of yesterday's priest of Atlantis.

Plato's picture of Atlantis shows us a mixture of beauty and ugliness, of wealth for some and slavery for others, of great riches defended by great armies and navies. Atlanteans were sailors,

A prehistoric statue of "The Lady of Elche," said to be a priestess from Atlantis.

It was said that Poseidon rose from the sea to become the father of the first Atlanteans.

traders, and fighters. They made bloody sacrifices to their god Poseidon who had come from the sea to make a good place for people to live. Their main city with its gold and silver temple atop a mountain, ringed by buildings and waterways, must have looked like a giant cake!

From Plato, we also know that the end of Atlantis came about 11,500 years ago. In the beginning it had been a place of peace, a place of beauty where people respected the truth and each other. But as time went by, the Atlanteans became greedy, violent people. They put pleasure before everything else. Legend says that Poseidon, unhappy about such a change, took Atlantis into the sea. But that's only legend.

Is all of Atlantis a legend? Did Atlantis exist? If we are to believe the ancient Greek story of Atlantis, why can they not tell us what happened to that mysterious land? If Atlantis did exist, *where is it now?*

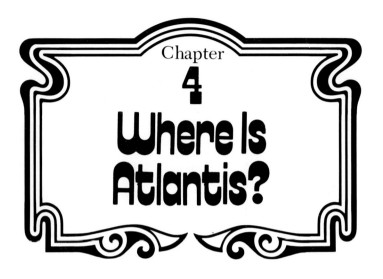

Chapter 4
Where Is Atlantis?

Imagine that one day a series of earthquakes followed by a huge tidal wave destroyed and swallowed the whole of Europe. That's right. You wake up one morning and where all of Europe used to be there is now a great hole filled with sea—perhaps a speck of land or two.

Now imagine what it might be like 10,000 years from today, looking for Europe and its glorious cities. Remember, there are no photographs or television tapes to help you. No history books or maps can be used to locate what used to be France or Germany. All you have to go by is the story of one person, long since dead, who has left his writings for you to find. Had this person ever *seen* the countries of Europe? No, only what others had seen and reported about Europe was known. Are these firsthand reports by people who, themselves, had been to Europe? No, it had vanished too long ago for there to be direct reports. We have only the stories that come from stories that come from the direct report.

Are you getting the idea of what it is to hunt for Atlantis or even to find clues as to *if* it was or *when* it was? The only evidence we have that Atlantis even existed at all comes from Plato. That's a very slim lead on which to solve a 10,000 year old mystery! But it's all we have, so let's continue the search for Atlantis.

How can a whole continent be lost? There has to be some trace. It's just that Atlantis is underwater, and traces are hard to find. Plato tells us that after the great flood, when Atlantis went under the sea, there were some very shallow water areas over the island's tallest mountains.

Today, reaching from off the coast of Africa to northeast of the West Indies there is a huge area of sea that lies very still. The winds don't blow there and an enormous patch of thick seaweed has grown up. When ships sailed between Europe and the new lands of America, they tried to avoid the area. Once into these calm, weed-choked waters, it took a very long time to get out

Ships have always had to fight the seaweed that chokes the Sargasso Sea.

again. It is called the Sargasso Sea—one of just two places in the world where a ship's compass points not to the magnetic north but to true north.

There is little or no wind for ships under sail in the Sargasso, and the seaweed makes it almost impossible to row out. Sailors who have been there say that the seaweed looks thick enough to walk upon. The Sargasso Sea is where Plato said the sunken Atlantis could be found. It's also the water that was too shallow for ancient ships to sail through after the flood. By itself, of course, the Sargasso Sea doesn't prove there was an Atlantis, but if the Sargasso weren't there, we might have reason to doubt Plato.

If you were to drain all the water from the Atlantic Ocean, so it emptied like a bathtub, you would find some very interesting things. First, you'd find that it isn't like a bathtub at all. The bottom of the ocean isn't flat. The continents of Africa, America, and Europe rise out of the water like the tops of great mountains that lie underwater.

Off the coast of Africa, there is a steep valley in the ocean floor. The valley is surrounded by some small mountains that rise sharply. The tops of these mountains rise out of the Atlantic. They are the Azores and Canary Islands. South of the North American shore, there is also a sharp valley. The mountains around this valley rise above the water to form the Bahamas, Cuba, and the West Indies.

If Atlantis really had been an island, like the Azores or the Bahamas, there should be a huge range of mountains right in the middle of the Atlantic Ocean floor. The mountains would probably be under what we call the Sargasso Sea. We now know there are such mountains. A huge, flat-topped mountain range, looking just like a continent, has been found right in the middle of the Atlantic. It is not high enough to be out of the water at all, but it rises 9,000 feet above the ocean floor. It runs approximately under the Sargasso Sea.

Now, our hunt for Atlantis seems to be going a bit better, doesn't it? A few more clues tell us Plato seems to have known what he was talking about. Something that looks very much like a continent is lying under the Atlantic Ocean, right where Plato said it was. But is it really Atlantis? Has any part of it ever been above the water? Does this undersea mountain show any sign of terrible destruction?

When the telegraph was invented, people were able to send messages to each other quickly, even over the ocean. All that was needed was to string a wire or cable across the ocean floor. Cables were laid underwater between America and Europe. One of these cables broke, and a crew was sent by ship to fix it. The cable break was about 500 miles north of the Azores, off the coast of Africa—right about where the sunken Atlantis should be. Divers repairing the cable had a difficult time under the water. They found the sea floor to be anything but flat. There were peaks and valleys, mountains, and other shapes.

The repair crew brought up samples of a black, glass-like lava. Lava is the hot, liquid rock that comes from the inner earth and out onto the earth's surface through a volcano. The liquid rock hardens and becomes like glass when it cools quickly in the air. If the lava cools underwater, it forms small crystals like sand. *Another clue in the mystery of Atlantis!* The lava found by the cable crew must have cooled *above* water. The mountains under the Sargasso Sea must have once been above the ocean!

Plato says Atlantis sank about 11,000 years ago. The lava samples brought back by the cable repair crew were found to be less than 15,000 years old. Once again, Plato is not proved wrong. At some time in the last 15,000 years, at least one volcanic mountain range must have sunk into the Atlantic Ocean, about where Plato tells us Atlantis was!

Another interesting clue was found when sand was brought up from the ocean bottom far

Does the "lunar landscape" on San Miguel Island, in the Azores, indicate great earth changes in the past?

off the coast of the Azores. The sand was found to be *beach sand*. Beach sand is rather special. It forms only from the action of waves beating against shells and rocks in shallow water. This was more proof that land once standing above the ocean water had, at some time, sunken many thousands of feet into the water. How else would beach sand cover the ocean floor at that point?

The green and blue lakes of Sete Cidades on San Miguel.

Are the clues in our mystery beginning to add up to an answer? A huge continent does seem to have sunk under the waves of the Atlantic Ocean almost 15,000 years ago. It does seem to have had plains and great mountain ranges, just as Plato described. There were beaches and harbors, now all underwater. It seems we know about *where* to look for Atlantis. But if we look further, will we find signs of Atlantis' cities that add proof to Plato's story?

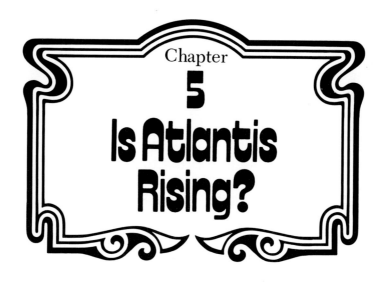

Chapter

5
Is Atlantis Rising?

Not long after Taylor Caldwell had her Atlantis dream, another famous writer also dreamed about Atlantis. His name was Edgar Cayce. He became famous because he often seemed able to tell the future. His life story is too long to tell here. But if you are interested, there are many books about the fantastic things Cayce saw in his dreams.

From about 1923 to 1944, Cayce's dreams were filled with stories of Atlantis. His dreams were so real to him that he made a prediction about Atlantis. He said that a temple of Atlantis would rise above the ocean water. The temple would appear off an island in the Bahamas called Bimini. Cayce said that it would happen in 1968 or 1969. As you can imagine, most people laughed at him. *A temple rising out of the sea—* and from Atlantis! Ridiculous!

In 1968, however, the world stopped laughing at Edgar Cayce's dream of a temple rising from the Atlantic deep. A commercial airline pilot claimed he saw it while flying over the Bahamas. The pilot says he looked down into the clear blue water, in about the area where Cayce said the temple would appear. There, underwater, was the clear outline of a building. The huge building looked like a temple! The pilot took pictures of what he saw.

Investigators flocked to the area around the Bahamas. Under the water they found great stone blocks fitted together to form a wall. The wall ran for miles. Can these great stones come from the Atlantis walls Plato talked about? Is it possible they are from an ancient Atlantis highway? We don't know.

Some legends about Atlantis say it was really two islands. These legends say one of the islands

Scientists say these huge stone blocks are ancient remnants of a wall, road, or harbor. Could they be from Atlantis?

was called Atlantis. This was the island close to Africa. The other island was called Poseida and is thought to have been closer to North America. If there were two Atlantis islands, is one island rising? Is it the one closest to North America, near the Bahamas? Until we have more evidence, we can't know. Perhaps one day *you* will be part of a team of Atlantis "detectives." Maybe *you* will be the one to solve the mystery of Atlantis.

Even more recently, searchers have found ruins under the sea off the coast of Spain. Again there are signs of great stone walls and buildings. Again they are just where Plato said they would be found. Unfortunately, the Spanish government prevented further exploration because the ruins are close to a modern naval base. It's very frustrating, isn't it, not to be able to take a closer look!

Was there a great mountain range surrounded by fertile plains that was swallowed by the sea? It certainly looks like it. Was it inhabited by a great people who sailed widely over the seas, trading and fighting and building a great empire? Perhaps. Is it Atlantis that is rising? No one knows. But the work of exploring the underwater mountains has only begun.

If there was an Atlantis, what was it? Was it the land where men built a beautiful place to live and then became ugly themselves? Was it the place that was swallowed in one day and one

47

night by a huge tidal wave? Whatever it was, perhaps Atlantis can tell us a lot about ourselves.

Perhaps Atlantis is only a dream—a dream of living in peace and plenty on this planet. If so, it is a dream worth holding onto. It tells us we must learn to overcome our jealousies and greed. That is a problem each of us must help to solve if our world is to survive. Remember, some dreams do come true. Perhaps the dreams of Edgar Cayce and Taylor Caldwell will come true. And hold on tight to your own dreams. They too could come true. *Maybe you'll even find your own Atlantis!*